Romance with God

ROMANCE WITH GOD

Aadil Farook

RESOURCE *Publications* • Eugene, Oregon

ROMANCE WITH GOD

Copyright © 2024 Aadil Farook. All rights reserved. Except for brief quotations in critical publications or reviews, no part of this book may be reproduced in any manner without prior written permission from the publisher. Write: Permissions, Wipf and Stock Publishers, 199 W. 8th Ave., Suite 3, Eugene, OR 97401.

Resource Publications
An Imprint of Wipf and Stock Publishers
199 W. 8th Ave., Suite 3
Eugene, OR 97401

www.wipfandstock.com

PAPERBACK ISBN: 979-8-3852-2348-0
HARDCOVER ISBN: 979-8-3852-2349-7
EBOOK ISBN: 979-8-3852-2350-3

VERSION NUMBER 05/22/24

Contents

The Rhythm Of 2022 | 1
The Veiled One | 4
The Rumi Within | 7
The Lost Crown | 9
The Existential Narration | 11
Conquer The World | 13
The Unanswered Question | 14
The Great Misconception | 16
The Dialog Of 2020 | 18
The Godless Delusion | 22
The Ummah's Cry | 24
Ode To Someone Special | 26
The Divine Music | 27
The Esoteric Song | 28
The Alchemy | 30
A Love Affair | 32
An Act Of Worship | 36
A Beggar In The Kingdom | 38
I, Revealed | 39
The God Of Sinners | 40
The Unsung Melody | 42
Nature & I | 44

The Riddle Of Life | 45

A Letter To God | 47

The Anthology of Ironies | 50

The Universal Quest | 52

Confessions Of Muhammad (pbuh) | 54

Fruits From A Prophetic Tree | 58

The Nursery Rhyme Of Adulthood | 60

[The Rhythm of 2022]

Will human nature ever change?
From devils to angels is its range
Can religion alone transform us
Without spirituality in the nucleus?
Does mere belief bring moral elevation?
If not accompanied by a firm conviction?

It's the cup of love that purifies humans
Eradicating the taint of inner demons
When you let love take control
There is a unity of body and soul
Love grants a fresh new start
Ends mind's war with heart

Love has higher reasoning
Way beyond logical thinking
When the grasp of rationality ceases
Our intuitive intelligence increases
Love has a lens that is so clean
Conceals that which makes us mean

Love has wings with a perpetual flight
Because it galvanizes our inner sight
Love is a domain with no boundaries
Its seeds always turn into trees
Love sees no pagans in people
Its reach is above good or evil

Love is the precondition of peace
Solves the puzzle piece by piece
Love is the oxygen of life
For existence without strife
Love is the symbol of beauty
It's the essence of humility

Love is the ultimate sign of God
An armor against any sword
Love conquers any philosophy
As its knot ties to divinity
Love is true like any Science
As it breeds no human bias
Love is the immortality of mortals
Bringing home the highest laurels
Love is the cornerstone of greatness
The secret behind immaculate success
Love unlocks the code of fate
Knowing best how to translate

Without love, Rumi was just a scholar
Before love, Ghazali was only a thinker
Love was the spark of Ibn-al-Arabi's genius
Without it, philosophy was Iqbal's Venus
When they tasted the depth of love
Wisdom opened its doors from above

Love isn't merely a four-letter word
In it lies a symphony to be heard
It is the emancipation of human-self
It is a library, not a shelf
Speeches, sermons theorize liberty
Love turns it into actuality

Let the world embrace this message
Towards cure, this is the passage
Let humanity dig much deeper
to discover our differences are meeker
May this be the rhythm of 2022
One day, let this poet's dream come true!

[The Veiled One]

How many veils must be lifted
till your glimpse is gifted
How much pride must be sacrificed
till your grandeur is recognized
How much tribulation must be undergone
till a purified self is born
How many desires must be forsaken
till I let my soul awaken
How much heartbreak must be felt
till I allow my ego to melt
How many wishes must be blown away
till my only wish is your say
How many tears must be shed
till my spirit is truly fed
How much knowledge must be unlearned
till your gnosis is to be earned
How many books must be burned
till your message is fully learned
How many reasons must bear negation
till your love is granted affirmation
How many temptations must be fought
till the distance between us is naught
How many wines must be untasted
till your vision turns me intoxicated
How many petals of 'I' must wither
till I am able to pluck your flower
How many colors of me must fade
till your rainbow is displayed

How many songs must be unheard
till, by your melody, I am stirred
How many peers must abandon me
till I am granted your proximity
How much jealousy must harm me
till I rely on only your sincerity
How many fears must be conquered
till your path is wholly traveled
How much self must be lost
till this journey is crossed

How many wars with myself must I win
till your disclosure will finally begin
How many words must be written
till silence becomes my expression
How many people must be forgiven
till I make my days enliven
How many memories must I erase
till my nights are for your praise
How many "why's" must be understood
till I experience what is selfhood
How many "how's" must be explored
till your divine wisdom is poured
How many theories must be rejected
till your concept is perfected
How much philosophy must I replace
till your discourse rules my space-time
How much science must be unendorsed
till the power of faith is the greatest force
How many illusions must be denied
till the devil's tricks are defied
How many steps must I walk
till your exaltation is my talk

How many delusions must be addressed
till with your revelation, I am blessed
How much should I strive for bliss
till prostration is like a bride's kiss

How much repentance must accompany sin
till I witness a revolution within
How much from vanity I must flee
till you acknowledge my humility
How much caprice must be suppressed
till you say, "I am highly impressed"
How much inner purity should I seek
till feminine beauty can't make me weak
How much worldly glitter must I shun
till your rays are emitted from the sun
How much should I serve your creation
till I fulfill the definition of a human
How much should I revere your glorious name
till the key to your treasures, I can claim
How much remembrance do I owe your beloved
till I'm mentioned in the prayers of the prophet
How much self-worship must be undone
till I'm embraced by you, the Veiled One!

[The Rumi Within]

Carve the path untraveled before
Let your spirit fly and roar
Your worth isn't a thousand or a crore
It is tied to the ideal you adore
Free yourself from mundane chores
Let your forehead kiss the floor
In your heart, let light pour
Slowly, open the divine door
Cling to the covenant you swore
Collect the pieces that you tore
Let God hear you implore
Not asking for anything more
Just the attire you once wore
Seek new vistas to explore
Love is a sea with no shore
Let it transform your core
The thought of vice, you'll abhor
With Satan, you'll settle the score
Your silent prayer, God won't ignore
You'll be gifted with a mentor
Let him be your salvor
Faith in virtue, he'll restore
Blessings will be galore
Hedonism, you'll deplore
Your selfhood will soar

Your bosom, a reservoir of compassion
Your mind, a decoder of gnostic station
Your eye, a witness to wonderment

Your soul, home to secrets' unfoldment
Your feet will learn ecstatic dance
With God, you will enjoy romance

O' Seeker,
It's time to erase the mark of sin
Embrace yourself with a new skin
Let the never-ending journey begin
There is no defeat or win
Neither enemy nor kin
In any way, your life can spin
If you don't fear any chagrin
You'll discover the Rumi within

The deeper you dive
In loneliness, you thrive
There's no fight to survive
Just strive, strive, and strive!

[The Lost Crown]

O' Muslims,
Where's the thought stirring the world?
Where's the intellect discerning God's word?
Where's the knowledge enlightening the West?
Where's the character passing every test?
Where's the morality spreading like fire?
Where's the spirituality taking you higher?
Where are the minds gifted with genius?
Where are the hearts with a pure nucleus?
Where's the civilization embellishing the earth?
Where's the scholarly ink of priceless worth?
Where's the wisdom tearing the veils of time?
Where's the grace making you sublime?
Where's the learning transcending all regions?
Where's the legacy of the soaring falcons?
Where's the power trouncing the forces of Satan?
Where's the progress without contradicting religion?
Where are the dreams coming true?
Where's the passion igniting you?
Where's the Salah being a believer's ascension?
Where's the ideology launching a revolution?
Where's the eye witnessing God's splendor?
Where's the gaze lowering in front of her?
Where's the mark of Ghazali's critiques?
Where's the pen that challenged the Greeks?
Where's the mystic of Ibn-al-Arabi's fervor?
Where's the literature with Rumi's flavor?
Where's the philosophy of Iqbal's vision?
Where's the gnosis of Wasif's precision?

Where's the unity defining brotherhood?
Where's the ideal elevating selfhood?
Where's the reverence for an insightful saint?
Where's the silence that's not a constraint?
Where are the women concealing beauty?
Where are the seekers radiating humility?
Where are the believers enthused by a global cause?
Where are the thinkers free from secular claws?
Where's the Science evolving from revelation?
Where's the brainpower serving the nation?
Where are the libraries with quiet readers?
Where are the books, the idea-breeders?
Where are the strategies defying the devil's plan?
Where's divine intervention empowering man?
Where's the sword being raised for Gaza?
Where's the poetry with faith-centric stanzas?
Where are leaders who can't forsake Sunnah?
Where are those proud to be slaves of Allah?
Where's the pain for the relinquished vicegerency?
Where are the tears in the nights of secrecy?
Where's the love for the entire humanity?
Where in the noise is the voice of sanity?
Where's the perfect blend of virtue and ability?
Where's the manifestation of Umer's personality?
Where are the souls unleashing divine mystery?
Where's the transformation unmatched in history?
Where's the will to enact God's system?
Where are those who are Islam's emblem?

If you seek glory in this world and the next
Follow Muhammad (pbuh) in spirit and text
His path would never let you drown
Embrace him to regain the lost crown!

[The Existential Narration]

Is life a supreme puzzle?
Is it an unsolved riddle?
Is it really a gift from God
or a test that cuts like a sword?
Is it actually the conquest of evil
or virtue's manifestation in a few people?
Is it the nurture of intellect in minds
or disclosure of emotions of all kinds?
Is it the drama that is simply too real
or the gradual opening of fate's seal?
Is it as organized as empirical science
or a random set of events with no signs?
Is it mere occurrence of tragedies for the pure?
Does it have an equalizer after its tenure?
Hasn't throughout history havoc been played?
Is it worth the price that was paid?
Is it only an opportunity for our talents' display
Or a chance to perform deeds that won't go away?
Is world peace only a utopian idea of the naive?
Hasn't this planet been chaotic since Adam & Eve?
Awful is the record of human nature
Is man the most superior creature?
Does religion unveil the mystery
or only plant a rootless tree?
Neither books nor experience gives answers
Knowledge is built on weak pillars
Mystics say that without a clean soul
Thought is deprived of the right role

Uncertainties diminish in the self's mirror
When man goes beyond philosophy's border
When he drowns in the divine love's ocean
When he tastes flavors unknown to reason
However, man cannot understand this
without being in that state's bliss
For most, this discourse makes no sense
But the reward of surrender is immense
I myself am stuck in that zone
where vanity hasn't yet blown
Maybe I will never attain that spiritual level
where hearts aren't corrupted by the devil
But I will always acknowledge my insignificance
In front of those who have gone the distance!

[Conquer the World]

Rise above daily chores
Throw inhibition on the floor
No more slavery to mundane deeds
Man is elevated when fully freed
From the goblet of life, pour in your heart
An endless stream of vigor to set you apart
Let every morning embrace new targets
Let your eyes be blind to all limits
Be numb to every impulse of fear
Meet each doubt with a haughty sneer
Though easy isn't the striving to excel
"Nothing is impossible", heroes tell
Greatness is the outcome of dreams
No matter how unrealistic it seems
Make your thirst the sole guidance
And perseverance, the only reliance
Sharpen the knife of your defining trait
Cut every hurdle that lies in your fate
Allow yourself to be challenged again and again
So your footsteps traverse an unwalked lane
Whether it is talent or virtue
Be such that others follow you
None of your indulgences is a vain venture
But a path toward a glorious future
Your every act shall be a beacon of inspiration
Each expression, a symbol of self-actualization
Let the diamond within you shine profusely
So your feat is hailed by all of humanity
Conquer the world, O aspiring champion
It's a mere jungle; you're the lion!

[The Unanswered Question]

Since the very dawn of mankind
it has baffled many a great mind
Why would God allow so much suffering?
The worldly show, is He really running?
The dynamics seem to contradict His attribute
and still, we must pay Him tribute
A gem cannot be polished without friction
Man cannot be perfected without tribulation
There's a reason why saints of every era
have found this life to be an enigma
On one hand, they are the ones most loved by Him
Yet, in a sea of affliction, they have to swim
Trials are proportional to man's status
Our true worth, they unveil to us
Only prophets are free from the need for purification
Their tests are nothing but for us a demonstration
They teach us the meaning of gratitude and patience
Why humans are the best of all creations
But what is manifested when man is spiritually ill?
Evil and injustice are the outcomes of free will
Or he would've been a mere puppet in God's hand
and his aspirations would be like castles of sand
But much deeper than that is the real mystery
if known, we won't challenge divine authority
What is the philosophy of our existence?
It is love God wants us to experience
which is impossible without pain's occurrence
just like darkness is to light's prevalence

If there was no grief on a planet like this
who would be inspired by heaven's bliss
Monotony is the other name for extinction and death
Change is the constant since time's first breath
God is extremely proud of His state of infallibility
So He confines this trait only for His own majesty
Human knowledge is of a very fragmentary nature
We will understand only upon meeting our Creator!

[The Great Misconception]

Have you ever wondered why the modern man
is in such conflict with the Divine plan?
Because he sees everything with the wrong lens
His distance from the truth is thus immense
He thinks every talent, skill or ability
is to earn nothing but personal glory
When he has quenched this desire of caprice
he feels it's the ultimate level of bliss
He calls it self-actualization
I label it self-destruction
No one is born with any faculty
that is a hindrance towards reality
How can God make someone into an actor or a dancer
when His teachings are to ensure none is a sinner
A single verse of the Quran can you quote?
or from the prophet's life, any anecdote?
which tells us that instead of piety
we should only strive for competency
The entire concept of religion
is under a spell of delusion
It is falsely said, "if you've got it, flaunt it"
God granted woman beauty but ordered her to conceal it
So tough is the path of humility
to not seek any worldly nobility

Spiritual masters aren't fools
to break contemporary rules
They always stress the lower-self's annihilation
Because in God's eyes, worth has a unique criterion
This isn't another philosophical contradiction
This is what I call the great misconception!

[The Dialog of 2020]

The search for truth has turned obsolete
For our caprice, social media is an ideal treat
No more time for lifting the veils on reality
Google is there to entertain us as its duty
Hedonism and consumerism thwart the human soul
That was created for a much higher goal
The pursuit of material progress and "prosperity"
Chokes a life of dimensions approaching infinity
Science and research cannot illuminate everything
Inner peace, technologies simply cannot bring
Philosophy has no potential to satisfy our quest
Art and literature distract us from voids at best
Political and economic isms have all been tried
In bridging theory with practice, they all lied
Religion has been confined to rituals or dogma
The journey within has become an enigma
The entirety of humanity is in crisis
Directionless, we strive for bliss
At will, the devils run the show
The seed of solution, none to sow
This planet longs for a magic wand
Or a new sun that hasn't dawned
That mortal can promise us salvation
In whom all qualities form a fusion

Only one man can save mother earth
To global welfare, he can give birth
His seeker cannot be at a loss
He's the secret behind this cosmos

Ages ago, his life did end
Yet, on his way, we depend
He showed path of divine light
He grants man his lost sight
He merged passion with vision
He indeed defines revolution
Claimants of his love are all around
But deeds like his won't be found
Believers hail him but don't follow him
Disbelievers are too blind to know him
In the West, his status isn't revealed
The East, without him, can't be healed
In the East, he is revered without imitation
The West criticizes him with no comprehension
Too far from his footsteps is the East
Enlightened or spiritual, the West is least
"Intellectuals", too arrogant to acknowledge him
The masses, too ignorant to understand him
The poor lack knowledge to walk his pathway
The rich surrender to their own desires' play
No conspiracy that he's vilified beyond measure
Tarnishing his legacy is the sick soul's pleasure
Yet the meaning of his name is "the praised"
Thus, from history, he cannot ever be erased
Among all giants, he alone is the king
His majesty makes me write and sing
Many hearts and minds exist in his dominion
His rule transcends any geographical region

O' beloved of God, none can ever be like you
Modern civilization, a drowning ship with no crew
Its indifference can't undermine your greatness at all
It would only increase its own perpetual fall

He who doesn't love your poverty
is not worthy of admiring your glory
He who hasn't seen your ascetic nature
should not see your grandeur either
He who can't appreciate your mystical aspect
should remain silent on your worldly impact
He who can't read your simplicity
is himself alien to what's humility
He who is unable to see your purity
is illiterate to the concept of beauty
He who doesn't surrender to your wisdom
is devoid of learning like the deaf & dumb
He who fails to feel your tears for all humanity
has no right to call you most influential personality
He who is unaware of your long prayers for the Ummah
Should not be impressed with your conquest of Makkah
He who can't see your perfection
is prey to Satan's deception
He who can't acknowledge you as a prophet
is comparing the sun to a candle being lit

Not recognizing you as the most exalted creation
is the negation of God's proudest affirmation
If God was a hidden treasure wanting to be known
The key to His heavens would be in your hands alone
The prayer that begins with your invocation
ends with the cosmic symphony's affiliation
The Muslims split into many factions without brotherhood
unite only to safeguard your finality of prophethood
The sword truly raised in only your name
is free from hatred, avarice and blame
Western thought says self-discovery comes after affirming ego
But you said that realization comes after negating ego
While modernity brought exploitation of nature

You taught that harmony is the vital factor
To uphold establishing peace without your reference
is concealing that love was your foremost reliance
Before space-time, when all souls endorsed God's existence
You had already been chosen as the leader of homo sapiens

O' Muhammad sallallaahu 'alayhe wa sallam
It is now time the world submits to you
It is now time the world submits to you
It is now time the world submits to you

And, due to heedlessness, if it doesn't
It will submit on the Day of Judgment
Here, you lived like a humble servant
There, everyone will be your servant!

[The Godless Delusion]

Be not baffled by the prevalence of many a smiling face
It is the perfect mask for the sorrow of the human race
How can a pain that is of a spiritual nature
be erased by indulgence in a physical venture?
The tragedy of man is that he has mistaken
momentary pleasure with true satisfaction
How can a mind full of falsity be at ease?
How can a blemished heart be at peace?
So much has been said on the concept of consciousness
Yet modern thought is devoid of intellectual finesse
Microscopic exploration of matter is the obsession
As if the spirit is in a state of recession
Is the quest for quenching never-ending curiosity
possible without comprehending ultimate reality?
These so-called sages claim to be path-seekers
Yet time unveils them as truth's disbelievers
Laborious learning of facts yields just information
But mystics gain special knowledge through intuition
Genuine bliss is indeed a very rare phenomenon
It's the fruit of intense self-transformation
Contemporary standards of success are ego-boosters
Endless inner voids turn us into imposters
How can ignorance of the self's need
give birth to a truly amazing deed?

When the soul is disconnected from its origin
Contentment is merely a theoretical description
Only once, I have experienced that ecstasy
that Sufis manage to possess perpetually
I can never deny that divine force
that links us to our actual source
As long as pure religion is deemed as life's rival
Pursuit of happiness will remain a vicious cycle!

[The Ummah's Cry]

Let the flower of sanguinity bloom
Whether the zephyr of conquest blows or not
Let the clouds of unity burst
Whether the rain of tranquility falls or not
Let the strings of struggle be plucked
Whether the melody of triumph echoes or not
Let the shades of brotherhood prevail
Whether the color of love forms or not
Let the sagacity of revelation rule
Whether intellect's grasp captures it or not
Let the wings of faith take you far
Whether reason's ascent reaches there or not
Let the fervor of heart behest you
Whether mind's consent is granted or not
Let the alchemy of religion transform you
Whether tribulation's heat melts you or not
Let your ship sail to the shore of sainthood
Whether the rock of calamity hits it or not
Let your eyes drown in tears
Whether your limbs sinned or not
Let the rhythm of Quran fail your senses
Whether your ears hear the beat or not
Let the words set your spirit ablaze
Whether the language estranges you or not
Let the verses carve endless paths in you
Whether your mortality bears it or not
Let the chapters unlock new vistas for you
Whether knowledge is expended or not
Let life's pendulum hinge on Sunnah
Whether the air lets it swing or not

Let yourself traverse Muhammad's path
Whether his footsteps are followed or not
Let his attributes envelop you
Whether you saw him or not
Let his lamentation stir you
Whether you heard it or not
Let salutation provoke him to greet you
Whether he is present or not
Let piety unseat talent
Whether prestige is bestowed or not
Let belief defy logic
Whether the world has changed or not
Let deeds engulf means
Whether space-time caters or not
Let yourself shatter the fetters of West
Whether you are mocked or not
Let a Sufi be mightier than a tyrant
Whether he is feared or not
Let holy warriors be as worthy as the genius
Whether they are envied or not
Let your soul wear the vicegerent's attire
Whether your body is worthy or not
Let your will write fate
Whether the Grand Pen has dried or not
Let the cosmos connive for you
Whether you knew it or not
Let your acts alter history
Whether prophethood is sealed or not
Let God rejoice in your creation
Whether the angels comprehend it or not
Let Him hail your existence
Whether Satan surrenders or not
Let He await your return
Whether you yearn for it or not
Let Him embrace your being
Whether you earned it or not!

[Ode To Someone Special]

Just when it all seems a dead end
and nothing is easy to comprehend
the damage is impossible to mend
Only failure, I apprehend
To my existence, misery appends
It seems futile to make amends
there are no prayers to ascend
to my cries, none will attend
No new person worthy to befriend
No one to advise or recommend
Of confusion, life is a blend
Fate becomes a rule I can't bend
My experience, no one to commend
Too many adversaries to contend
Everyone wants to offend
My rights, no one to defend
No more blessings to descend
Upon anything, I can't depend
No more energy to expend
No boundaries to transcend
No open arms to extend
No virtue to intend
Not even a penny to spend
Fears and doubts, I can't suspend
Success is a myth, a bygone legend
A single smile, I can't pretend
And tragedy has become a trend
Waiting for me is someone only God can send
She is my mother, my angel, my best friend!

[The Divine Music]

Go way beyond the reach of mere logic
For once, identify your soul is sick
Beware of the genius of Satan's trick
Be moved by your conscience's prick
Shun arguments of that shallow critic
who doesn't know the path of a mystic
In the wall of love, be that brick
which none can remove or pick
Whether life is joyous or tragic
Whether truth is simple or ironic
No occurrence will make you frantic
Fear is turned off by a single click
Let this world not turn you nostalgic
No matter if it seduces you with gimmick
Bookish knowledge can't guarantee magic
Unveiling becomes slower than a clock's tick
Beat your carnal self with that stick
which transforms a scholar into a gnostic
whose speech isn't of a usual cleric
but is preserved as a museum relic
He is devoid of the desire to be iconic
Yet becomes virtue's unrivaled yardstick
The prophet's shoes, let your tongue lick
so you, finally, hear the Divine Music!

[The Esoteric Song]

O' ostentation
Vanish. I am about to write
O' fame
Approach me not. I know my intent
O' pride
Leave me. I am beautiful without you
O' ego
Runaway. I have chosen innocence
O' people
Silence. My will isn't your dictation
O' world
Don't entice. My self is pure indeed
O' Nafs
Surrender. Your fate is slavery to me
O' Satan
Give up. Love has outplayed intellect
O' jealousy
I am contented with what I have
O' anger
Humility taught me to overcome you
O' lust
My definition of beauty has changed
O' power
My strength lies in weakness before your Owner
O' path
No philosopher am I to be ignorant of your secrets
O' cosmos
I am not a scientist to reckon you a mystery

O' knowledge
The disciple in me learned that you could be a veil
O' Muhammad
I seek you in every master, but none approaches you
O' God
I pray that this isn't narcissism in disguise!

[The Alchemy]

No God am I to define evil and good
Yet man enough to express selfhood
By Aadil, I want love to be understood
and wish to burn like a piece of wood
I yearn to see beyond space and time
Worldliness is but a spiritual crime
I crave the shattering of norms
For breaking inhibition in all forms
Enough of living without an inspired philosophy
Adherence out of fear doesn't bring any trophy
It is love that dispels myths of reason
It reveals the self's hidden dimension
It unveils the sacred nature of a human
Being unmoved by the body's deception
It fully lifts every curtain
Divine Presence will ascertain
Because the heart is its source of cognition
It's the cause behind soul's ignition
It fosters that special everlasting ideology
where coherence is the only terminology
where seeking the Truth isn't a game of chess
Reality is clear as a sun's morning caress
Man rises above daily chores
In the seventh sky, he soars
Welcoming even the tribulation
as an opportunity for elevation
In his dictionary, every word carries a positive connotation
His mind traverses the spectrum of faithless speculation

Then he is granted that secret password
No image of existence is left blurred
He is that evidence endorsing God's own breath
This is the consequence of one's ego's death
Discursive language is devoid of transcendence
To encapsulate concepts of such essence
This experience culminated in holy prophet's ascension
whose self didn't need further transformation
He was closer to God than two lovers in a kiss
No mortal in history came nearer than this!

[A Love Affair]

You are the rainbow of infinite shades traversing the entire sky
I am just an eye filled with the wonder of your sight
You are the queen enjoying the grandeur of a palace
I am just a gem proud to be a part of your crown
You are the sun defying the existence of night
I am just a particle of a single ray
You are the melody of a symphony of Beethoven
I am just an eardrum captivated by your sound
You are the trophy after an impossible victory
I am just a beat of the heart filled with joy
You are the peak of Mount Everest
I am just a stone displaced from the surface
You are the philosophy of life
I am just a thought behind an argument
You are the scientist unveiling mystery of the cosmos
I am just a tiny corner in your laboratory
You are the passion in a bride's first kiss
I am just the intention before a flirtatious gaze
You are the face of the most beautiful woman
I am just a concealed scar on her foot
You are the stratagem of a leader
I am just the advice of a servant
You are the devotion beneath an angel's prostration
I am just a piece of cloth under his brow
You are the regret at the time of death
I am just a sigh of discomfort
You are the purity of a mother's affection
I am just the infatuation of a teenager
You are the poetry of Shakespeare

I am just a song verse once played on the radio
You are the grace of Michael Jackson's performance
I am just a dance move of a wedding ceremony
You are the addiction of a drug
I am just a habit left off
You are the intensity of human ego
I am just a feeling of doubt
You are the deception of spectacular magic
I am just a mirage on the road
You are the thirst of a desert traveler
I am just the last sip of a drunkard
You are the reason for a nation's creation
I am just another citizen of the country
You are the calmness of a gigantic ocean
I am just the fragility of a drop of water
You are the selflessness of a martyr
I am just a pleasant gesture of an acquaintance
You are the certainty of a scholar
I am just a preacher's opinion
You are the humility of a saint
I am just an emotion behind a salutation
You are the will of perseverance
I am just a desire for success
You are the gratitude of a Sufi
I am just an expression of "thank you"
You are the gift of genius
I am just an acquisition of talent
You are the sparkle of a spring
I am just a morning splash of water
You are the taste of the finest chocolate
I am just a spoonful of sugar
You are the perfection of a champion
I am just an infrequent practice
You are the desperation of a beggar

I am just the motivation for a chore
You are the thrill of finding buried treasure
I am just the discovery of a coin on the ground
You are the stability of the wall of China
I am just a brick in a laborer's hand
You are the holy book of a revealed religion
I am just a speck of dust on a library shelf
You are the prophetic prayer longing to change the world
I am just a letter of one word uttered
You are the fabric of time and space
I am just a fleeting moment
You are the conclusion of truth
I am just a perception of reality
You are the chastity of Rabia Basri
I am just the shyness of a virgin
You are the clandestine of God
I am just an occurrence in fate
You are the sacred tradition
I am just another rite
You are the breeze of paradise
I am just another fragrance
You are the intuition of a sage
I am just the guess of a child
You are the zenith of expression
I am just another smile
You are the pinnacle of nearness
I am just another embrace
You are the light of God's disclosure
I am just a flame about to fade
You are the courage of a warrior
I am just a mimicry of confidence
You are the authenticity of love
I am just an instant of sensuality
You are the fervor of a revolution

I am just a wish for betterment
You are the pragmatism of Jinnah
I am just a dream of a poet
You are the meaning of existence
I am just a phenomenon to undergo change
With splendid colors
I painted the image of our love
You have captured the artist
Never throw the picture away!

[An Act of Worship]

Oh, this is such bliss
like a bride's first kiss
Finally, I put my head into prostration
and swallow my pride without frustration
At last, I lift my hands for a prayer
my plea crosses the sky's seventh layer
I confess my intellect's actual triviality
and take the road leading to humility
I open the holy book for answers to questions
and nullify the devil's perturbing suggestions
Nothing can stop this spiritual quest
Man's superiority, even angels attest
The time has come to capture moments of joy
and feel like a child with a brand-new toy
No more misery, guilt and regret
Just God's graciousness to interpret
In front of Him, the more you're humble
In front of others, the less you stumble
If I seek no worldly reward
I may have truly found God
Pakistan chants, "go Nawaz go"
I say fight with your own ego
Give your caprice a big blow
Make your heart whiter than snow
Contrary to the common opinion
Love is the essence of religion

Now, I may be deemed as human
because this is my real origin
In the sea of myself, I was a warship
This sudden peace is an act of worship!

[A Beggar in the Kingdom]

Do I proclaim to serve you?
Servantship is riddance of all claims
Why call myself a believer?
My belief in dearth is sustenance
Can I call you my best friend?
I can disclose none to the All-Knowing
Would I ever grasp your splendor?
I can lose all but mortality
Should I find you beyond stars?
I haven't yet discovered you within
Can I express your beauty?
Words aren't born since eternity
Shall I confront your vision?
The purest of hearts be bathed thrice for it*
Do I wish to be humble?
My heart betrays my head in prostration
Do I dare to fear you?
I haven't broken all idols yet
Could I deem life as owned?
I possess not even that I breathe
Can I claim love for you?
Its division is an attribute of others
Am I in submission to you?
I would've preferred worship over poetry

Will I be granted heaven or hell?
Both are one
Till your curtain is raised!

*Muhammad (pbuh) during ascension (miraaj)

[I, revealed]

Sins, the only souvenir of my past
Guilt, the enduring friend

Ego, the queen of my palace
Lust, the only stone of my castle

Indulgence, my only persistence
Lament, the only salvation

Self, the only compass guiding me
Indifference, the only escape

Taint, the only fingerprint
Loss, my only signature

God, the outtake from my wish list
Angels, the only repellant

Possessions, my only bounty
Blessings, the only dispossession

Burden, the only one to carry me
Fear, the only lift

Darkness, the only shade
Change, the path uncrossed

Actions, the most wanted weapon
Words, the only shot left!

[The God of Sinners]

The earth vows to swallow us
yet calmed
it's His kingdom only

The waters simmer to sink us
their rage humbled
it's between He and us

The air is perpetually charged
held starved nonetheless
He knows the unknown

The angels beseech for our death
their hopes buried
He sees what they don't

The nights promise malevolence
their claims beset
It's He or none

The clouds dare to own thunder
their threats threatened
none exists unless He intends

The lightning grows monstrous
all fears erased nevertheless
who else is the King?

The sun yearns to scorch us
the phenomena seized
none stirs without His will

The sky declines to light up
the moon defies it
each star salutes none but the Master

The mountains linger to demolish us
their swelter frozen
none erupts unless His vehemence

Gabriel warns to conclude it all
his roar silenced
all is mortal but the Immortal

But the devils within go on satirizing
He smiles back
only He discerns the idiocy beneath

Still, we cling on to merriment
His smile fades
only He writes our epilogue.

[The Unsung Melody]

Truth is drowned in a sea of irrelevance
Falsity has worn the attire of reason

I am fooled by the illusion of freedom
Seduced by the winds of change

I've turned into a formless water
a trackless eagle with wings alone

My lips are sealed by the air of indifference
I am bound by the chains of conformity

Every day brings a vision unmet
Every night carries a task unfulfilled

Lies within me
a storm of emotions
an endless rain of thoughts
mounts of intentions

Yet I own nothing but words
Words that possess
neither the sting of swords
Nor the impact of hands
nor the march of footsteps
just words

But

there would've been neither an Ali
nor an Abu Bakar
neither an Umar
nor Muhammad
if they had words alone!

[Nature & I]

A drop perturbs the pond's serenity
a tear razes the peace of my heart
the drop's caress bares what's beneath
the tear unleashes tales unheard of
due to fragility, soon the ripples fade
owing to callosity, my eyes dry quickly
as myriad drops mingle into one
sundry scripts become one story
waters don't turn arid
and tears are no fluke
The sky's tint draws my own despair
The rainbow flaunts roles of my play
Lushness of fields brings me forged smiles
Hanging nights carry signs of my burdens
Moonlight's color is defied by its severity
The minority of tears deceives its own pain

Just as days and nights
carve a path for the sun
Birth and loss of tears
raise me and then make me fall.

[The Riddle of Life]

Learn till knowledge laughs
Pray till God loses clemency
Walk till routes are untraceable
Strive till struggles betray
Hope till miracles embrace nature
Seek till secrets finally yield
Sleep till you see your dream
Cry till you run out of sorrow

Shine fortunes under dim stars
Put verve in paralyzed souls
Wear wrinkles of labor, not age
Taste high with its reward's drug
Follow footsteps of changed paths
Be not haunted by ghosts of success
but always long for their visions

Before any volcano erupts
your lava shall melt it away
Before every love dawns on you
your sun should greet it earlier
This world has now grown
into a shriveled, dry rose
You be the first raindrop
kissing its dying petals

With fibers of your soul
paint the image of life
Destiny may throw the picture
but can't steal the artist
Never leave your people in ruins
Weren't angels enough for worship?

Though open, remain unpredictable
as a false desire that may stray
or a fed curse which can stay
be cold as a law
but appealing as a sin
sweet like playfulness
yet strong as a ruling motive
and as smooth as your death.

[A letter to God]

Love was my terrain
I was captured by you
Love was my kingdom
I was ruled by you
Love was a seduction
You were my indulgence
Love was a beauty
You were the sensation
Love was poetry
You were the fire
Love was my art
You were the madness
Love was genius
You were the spark
Love was sustenance
My survival was you
Love was my soul
You nourished me
Love was elevation
I fell for you
Love was a feat
You were my failing
Love was my performance
Its perfection was you
Love was a victory
My glory was you
Love was a crown
I was hailed by you

Love was hidden
Yet revealed you
Love was a garb
I wore you
Love was intoxication
You took me higher
Love was the guidance
But I followed you
Love was a sound
with echoes of you
Love was a cloud
You rained on me
Love was wealth
I earned you
Love was a possession
My treasure was you
Love was my freedom
Yet a slave to you
Love was a river
I drowned in you
Love was my grave
Yet buried in you
Love was a religion
My certainty was you
Love was a prayer
Its heart was you
Love was a prophet
my salvation was you
Love was my deity
I was blessed with you
Love was a life
My breath was you
Love was a friend
I was nurtured by you

Love was an embrace
I held on to you
Love was the sun
Yet a shadow to you
Love was time
Commenced with you
Love was a truth
Its reality was you
Love was an eternity
The existence was you.

[The Anthology of Ironies]

Could the ring of life be held
circles don't commence or end
From yourself, can you run
if spirit and body are one
Is it love if at you God stares
Yet in front, He never appears
Can joy survive without pain
Lovers call it a broken chain
Why care for blame or credit
You are not the world's pivot
Does the drunkard lose his sense
last sip gives him calm, immense
Can fireworks let a morning dazzle
Can paled rainbows grant splendor
Isn't the rousing of dawn caressed
when the night had rung silenced
while surrounding you, is air a companion
when it blew away, did you lose someone
Be it a diamond necklace or a cloth ribbon
for a dog, both are collars to kill freedom
Can you take off chastity never worn
Or hear in beloved's whisper a roar
Is love without beauty a fool's myth
or affirmed by an old lady's warmth
But isn't love overthrown by beauty
if nature enchants you with its bounty
can piety illuminate a heart's night
original colors are revived by light

Do you prefer loneliness over enmity
Fishes tremble outside water, clean or dirty
Is there a change in the lines on your palm
When every occurrence turns into harm
Shall you greet death with welcome
if an emotional seesaw, you become
Can we label our life as a friend
it won't leave us before the end
Could the angel of death be disloyal
Alike he treats beggars or royals.

[The Universal Quest]

Walk not on water yet
Stand firm on His ground
Trace not paths soon
Show Him hunger first
Climb not in air to reach sky
Your deeds must earn Him
Try not to move mountains
Till you fall for Him alone

Look not for shelter above
Let Him be the storm in you
See not the brightness of stars
He'll blind you to darkness
Aspire not to go distances
With Him you own the end
Fear never the journey left
He'll turn trees into towers

Say not a word with tongue
Let the heart speak to Him
Strive not to look beyond
Let your wonder see Him

Listen not to melodies around
Grant an ear to His Symphony
Write not your own songs
Make Him the rhythm of you

Dwell not why shall you know
He doesn't deprive the naive
Give not all you have
You lose Him in doing so
Strive not to prove anything
Success is failure to claim Him

Grow not roses of love
Let Him shield the garden first
Wait not for petals to blossom
Till His water runs through it

Wear not morning smiles
Till His sun rises for you
Endeavor not to prolong days
Till His moon shines for you
Wish not for a goodnight kiss
Till His dawn caresses you

Draw not horizons yet
Till He holds your hand
Catch not the world at once
Till He embraces you alone

Wipe not tears from eyes
Heal broken hearts for Him
Take not everyone in arms
Till you are touched by Him

Words are a mirror to us
Poetry isn't a gift to Him.
Salvation is our own need
Love is no tribute to Him!

[Confessions of Muhammad PBUH:
His Imaginary Tribute to God
on *Miraaj* (Ascension)]

If your entire mystery be reached
You be engraved in my destiny
If clouds of thoughts be held
You be every figment of my mind
If bursts of emotions be stirred
You be an endless valley in me
If a silent deep aura be created
I be numb to everyone else
If verve of my heart be foreseen
All my breaths, preserved for you

If windows of heaven be opened
your scent be known to me
If I had written revelations
your words be not poured in me
If echoes of divinity be escaped
I be deaf to your voice
If ironies be run from
I be sightless of your light
If autumn be deprived of its trait
all my secrets be unshed for you

If similarity in disparity be proven
your face be seen in my mirror
If equality be likened to inequality
myself in your presence be shown
If two unequal halves be created

only one of us completes the other
If precision of intuition be described
your silence discerned more than speech

If grains in Gabriel's palm be counted
My moments in your awe be reckoned
If span of East and West be traversed
horizon of your visions be marked
If mountains be separated from might
I be compared to my obsession
If oceans be poured into one goblet
my heart for you be unconcealed
If fire without spark be claimed
my state on your sight be revealed

If matter's inferiority to nature be judged
Aisha's ears not her diamond be seen
If wealth's triviality before love be proved
gold strands be replaced by Fatima's smiles
If the bliss of touch be expressed
Khadija's fingers be rested in mine
If bond of proximity be explained
Abu Bakar be locked in my arms

If a fiber be displayed to the seraphs
Bilal's shoelace be bestowed in heaven
If unity of souls be comprehended
Let Ali never be deprived of me
If the fervor of Umar be rivaled
my insanity without you be shown
If perfection be formed from amorphousness
I disbelieve in Yousaf's humanness
If Daud be inspired to sing
your glimpse be shown to him

If fragility of human senses be unlocked
my defense on your disclosure be shown
If women be unsaved from voracious eyes
Your unveiling be my only plead
If enrichment without decoration be denied
your freedom from embellishment lingers
If pinnacle of covetousness be bared
the moon be asked on your adornment

If outcomes of wars be rewritten
I be ending each as your captive
If sanctity of culture be preserved
I be holding you as the only ritual
If martyrdom be the aspired act
I be cherishing submission to you
If loyalty be proposed after death
The will of my phantom is yours

If Moses' failure to stand you be sensed
the glow of your face be confronted
If disbelief be merged with worship
my inner prostration be under trial
If extremity be adopted for once
every man be shunned as profane
If one blasphemy be forgiven
no prophet served you well
If Godhood be mine
Adam be punished as much as Iblis
If atheism be challenged ruthlessly
my own station be most at stake

If division of love and lust be refused
this poem's authenticity be doubted
If impurity be dropped into intentions
My failure be to write for someone else
If humility be separated from greatness
My presumption be to have done justice
If an angel be enticed towards a sin
My fear be to provoke vanity within
If an eruptive storm be submerged
in my confession, I be incapable
If something be ended before completion
Forever, my pen remain devoid of ink

If possessions be distinguished from wants
The pain of our separation be foreseen
If immortality of humans not resisted
my struggle for your consent subsisted

If one thing be changed about me
My being may not return to earth
If one thing be changed about you
the phenomenon of change be defied.

[Fruits From a Prophetic Tree—An ode to Muhammad SWS]

I may enhance my grandeur
but your majesty is the king
I may never be emancipated
but your honor is the fixation
I may relish to own everything
but your comfort is the earning
I may hunger for applause
but your call is the ascent
I may battle for supremacy
but your heart is the empire
I may envy a queen for her palace
But your companionship is the bliss
I may be wasted in aims afar reach
But your stature is the endeavor
I may bequeath jewels in a museum
But your foot's dust is the memento
I may undergo spells of ecstasy
But your presence is the elation
I may doubt charm's blend with worth
But your instance is the verdict
I may be immune to demons
But your embrace is the lure
I may float on a water torrent
But your eyes make me drown
I may be unmoved by ambiance
But your fragrance is the envelope
I may fetch Zamzam from Makkah
But your sweat is the relic

I may trust purity of Mikael's glance
But your emergence is the measure
I may do everything for a return
But your tolerance is the crave
I may wish to become a poet
But your delight is the reward
I may see Divinity in mortals
But your creation is the Art
I may succumb to Izrael anytime
But your death is the exception
I may yearn to glorify God
But your praise is the way!

[The Nursery Rhyme of Adulthood]

When friends turn into foes
and the river of agony flows
When hearts turn to stones
we become but flesh and bones
When souls are set on fire
with vengeance, a blazing desire
When humans turn into beasts
odium remains their only feast
When nectar of amity is sealed
Yet taste of jealousy is revealed
When the seed of trust is sown
But the tree of spite is grown
When candor is surmised as idiocy
Acumen lies in a mold of hypocrisy
When the voice within falls asleep
And the ocean of lust runs deep
When virtue is thrown or sold
And the sins are seen as gold
When you climb the mount of vice
But crawl on the road to paradise
Prayer is reckoned as mark of weakened
Mask of deceit won't unfold conceit
Hope is deemed a daft man's dream
Love is lost like a coin never tossed
Should we cling to the rope of belief?
Or is faith a tired man's relief?
Is God of this kingdom really there?
Does He play the game of life fair?

I bleed yet breath
I undergo anguish but don't relinquish
To the devil's whims, I won't surrender
And this sense of triumph is so tender
Neither I'll weep nor wish to fight
I want to eye with the inner sight
I am not a saint or a sage
Just someone at odds with the age!

www.ingramcontent.com/pod-product-compliance
Lightning Source LLC
Chambersburg PA
CBHW061247040426
42444CB00010B/2286